The Depths of Her: Through the Ashes

Britanee Webb

BookLeaf
Publishing

India | USA | UK

Presentation by *BookLeaf Publishing*

Web: www.bookleafpub.com

E-mail: info@bookleafpub.com

ISBN: 9789358318135

First edition 2023

DEDICATION

This book is dedicated to everyone in my life that brought these emotions to life through these words. Thank you for the lessons. With love.

Exist

I take a deep breath
And that's enough
I look up to the sun
And that's enough
I admire the moon
And that's enough
I adore the stars
And that's enough
I exist as I am
And that's enough

Help

She was all too familiar with internal battles
The ones that left deep wounds
For years memories rattled
Bottles and bottles she stored deep inside
Secrets she's kept
Emotions she hides
Though her demons kept her company it wasn't
welcome company to keep
And even with them there the loneliness went
deep
So much pain and sadness alone she felt
All because she didn't know how to ask for help

Keep Going

She never took the easy road to heal
It was never, pick your head up and keep going
for her
For her, it was fall, break, kick, cry, scream, feel
like you're going to die, THEN...
Pick your head up and keep going.
She had to feel it all because if she didn't it
would creep back in.
So, she chooses
Feel everything
Whole heartedly
Let it go
Pick your head up
Keep going

You

Years alone to mend her soul
She finally started to shine
In your darkness, you saw her light
She thought it was a sign

She told you to be careful
She's broke too many times
You said, "I got this"
You're also tired of the lies

And so they began to build
The life they always wanted
And though there were always smiles
Their pasts remained haunted

Truth pushed its way through the door
Destroying everything in its path
You dropped her beautiful heart
Here comes the aftermath

Aftermath

The aftermath of you
Reminded her of everything she worked to
forget
But if you ask her
It showed her where she hadn't been yet

It's time to get to work, she said
We have some things to fix
Chin up, straighten your crown
That's the last time things slip

Your heart is beautiful
And yes it can make a mess
But when you look back
Do you really have any regrets?

I Didn't Deserve It

I didn't deserve your dishonesty
I didn't deserve your transgressions
I deserve loyalty
I didn't deserve to be your possession

I didn't deserve the pain
I didn't deserve the tears
I deserve kindness
I didn't deserve the fear

I didn't deserve the mind games
I didn't deserve the bruises
I deserve a deep burning flame
I didn't deserve the excuses

I didn't deserve it
But by staying, the acts I allowed
I didn't deserve it
Now I stand my ground

Fallout

I try not to think about the signs I missed
Because now it seems so obvious

The signs missed are a path to the abyss
Please don't be oblivious

I've been there before, what's once more
There can't be anything I haven't seen before

Come on! You promised! Nevermore!
Stop! Don't go there! Come on, you swore!

So, what do I do now with the voices so loud
My brain is being plowed, it's like I'm being
drowned

Stop. Breathe. Remember what you're about.
Love. Always. Regardless of the fallout.

Free

I'm still learning to love the sad parts of me
The parts that couldn't see
All she was meant to be

The me that didn't understand
Everything I AM
And the parts of the world still unseen

The me who believed if I was good to you
You'd be good to me
And we'd all live happily

The me that ignored inconsistencies
To fade the deficiencies
I thought everyone could see

But don't you see?
The lies you tell yourself
The lies you continue to believe

The lies that keep you
From being free

Fear

9

Inside reactions to outside actions
What's the real issue here?

You're sad cause they don't "like" you
What do you really fear?

Fear….is a liar.
And you'll believe it if you don't watch out

"I can't do it"
"I'm not good enough"
WATCH WHAT YOU TELL YOURSELF!

She Knew

As broken as she seemed
In the current state of things
She knew there was light to be found

Though she can't see
And the dark is a scary place to be
She knew eventually she'd make ground

But at times she forgot
The light an afterthought
And she knew where this would lead

So she'd turn back around
Two feet on the ground
Because she knew it isn't as dark as it seems

Perfect Tragedy

I went on an adventure
To find what I had lost
All the pieces I left behind
On all the paths I crossed
Though I was prepared
For the dangers I'd face
I'd be lying if I said I wasn't scared
But determined to find every place
The places that I lost
The pieces of me
To put back where they belong
Free from the debris
The debris of casualty
Of what once was
Now a perfect tragedy
Because look what I've become

For the Life of Me

For the life of me
Did I ever think I'd be
Where I am currently

For the life of me
Did I ever think I'd be
Here, again, happy and hurting

For the life of me
Did I ever think I'd be
Once again yearning

Yearning for peace
Internally please
For the life of me

Learning to love me for me
Learning to be free
For the life of me

Disasters

Her healing created disasters. A real big mess of
things. Yes, those things would have to be
cleaned up along the way. It's what she did, and
man were her disasters beautiful. But let me tell
you, if you get the chance to see the outcome, if
you get to see what her beautiful disaster
created…
You would be in disbelief. It's what she does…
Creates beautiful disasters to put herself back
exquisitely

I'll Do Better

14

I'm sorry to my heart
I made you weak
I'm sorry to my voice
I didn't allow you to speak
I'm sorry to my soul
For the times I did not listen
I'm sorry to my body
For the times I didn't give permission
I'm sorry to me
For not being a boundary setter
I'm sorry to me
I promise I'll do better

Fork in the Road

15

Fork in the road
Which way to go
To be honest
Nobody knows
Just give it all you got
Whichever way you choose
You got one shot
And nothing to lose
Go with your whole heart
That's the only way face it
You got one life
Stop thinking so much before you waste it

Unread

Sometimes my truth doesn't always come out right. It can come out harsh and angry, but I promise I don't want to fight. I just get scared of how you'll react when I say that I am bothered. So, when it comes out, it spews out, and then it gets awkward.
Let me stop. Forget everything I said.
My truth gets tabled. Left unread.

Illusional

She always put so much pressure on herself
Which made no sense
She knew she'd never reach perfection
Nobody can
So why is she constantly trying to live up to her
own illusional expectations?
Who taught her that?
Somebody should really tell her it's time
It's time to let go and just be
Free of expectations that limit your beliefs
You're enough the way you are child
Not who you pretend to be

Me

When you're like me, seeing different
perspectives comes easily
But at some point I lost me and I didn't know
which perspective was me. You see, for me it
was hard, I didn't understand why I was always
on guard. But then, 'the yard', daddy hit me
cause I didn't agree so HOW was I supposed to
be…me. How was I supposed to be me when
you didn't let me. 'You know what's best for
me' but you didn't tell me.. WHY? Explain your
perspective then listen to mine. NOPE! Go to
your room. You're grounded. Bye!

The Mind

I kept it all in
Now it's all coming out
Wounds wide open
Hoping I won't bleed out

I've done it before
I can do it once more
I just didn't want to
I can't take it. War.

The thoughts in my head
Are pushing to the edge
They want me dead
To step off the ledge

But calm down, take a breath
You know what to do, you've done this
Yes, it feels like a living death
But you also know what the outcome is

Whole

Healing is a journey
No one showed her how to do it
From the scars and the fears
To the wounds and tears
She never thought she would get through it

She sat alone for months
No one had a clue
That at night she cried
As the old her died
And the light started to shine through

Day by day, piece by piece
She picked up her broken soul
She washed away
The years of pain
In time she will be whole

On Paper

Why is everything you write so depressing?

Um. Hello. Life isn't always nice. People aren't always kind. And no, my words don't always rhyme, but I'm real ALL the time. And mannn… shit hurts and sometimes I don't take it well. But when I put words on paper I come out of my shell. I can breathe. The weight is falling off of me. Life isn't so heavy. And I know I'm not the only one feeling this way.. I just chose not to hide the pain… on paper anyways.

www.ingramcontent.com/pod-product-compliance
Lightning Source LLC
Chambersburg PA
CBHW071255140726
47996CB00007B/2853